THE BERLIN WALL 1961-1989
Photographs from the stock of the Archives of the Land of Berlin

D1308833

THE BERLIN WALL 1961-1989

Photographs from the stock of the Archives of the Land of Berlin
Selected and commented on by Volker Viergutz

BERLIN STORY VERLAG

Imprint

Archives of the Land of Berlin (Editor):
The Berlin Wall 1961-1989
Sixth edition – Berlin: Berlin Story Verlag 2010
DVD: The Berlin Wall 1961-1989
        Authentic film documents including English commentary
        Total playing time 50 minutes (FSK 0)
ISBN: 978-3-929829-93-8

© Berlin Story Buchhandlung & Verlag
Unter den Linden 26, 10117 Berlin
Tel.: (030) 20 91 17 80
Fax: (030) 20 45 38 41
www.BerlinStory.de, E-Mail: Service@BerlinStory.de
Cover and typesetting: Tanja Zanolli-Saeger
Translated from the German by E.F.S. Zbikowski

WWW.BERLINSTORY.DE

Introduction

On August 13, 1961, the German Democratic Republic divided Berlin in two with a 95-mile-long wall which also isolated the three Western sectors from the surrounding area of Brandenburg. The GDR did this in order to put an end to the stream of refugees leaving East Berlin and the DDR, which had increased sharply in the preceding years and especially the preceding months. With this book of photos, the Archives of the Land of Berlin and the publishing company Berlin Story wish to recall a particularly dramatic period in the history of Berlin and one of the most abominable walls man ever built, and which left its imprint on the divided city for 28 years – from 1961 to 1989.

On May 26, 1952, the GDR closed the line of demarcation with the Federal Republic of Germany and the border with West Berlin. This was done to protest against the signing of the Germany Treaty, under which the three Western allies allowed greater sovereignty to the Federal Republic. The "green line" separating the two Germanies, open until then, was sealed off with barbed wire and a no-go strip. Berlin was also affected by these measures. Of the 178 streets which, until May 1952, linked West Berlin to East Germany or the GDR, 63 were closed just in the following days by the GDR authorities. The three Western sectors were in large measure sealed off from the surrounding countryside, and one had to reckon with identity checks when crossing the border within the city. Despite all this, the Western sectors of the quadripartite city of Berlin remained the last refuge which could be reached with relatively little risk by taking the commuter train or by using the still-open streets to cross the border – until 1961.

The stream of refugees from the GDR increased from year to year due to 1) the failure of the popular uprising of June 17, 1953, 2) the catastrophic economic situation resulting from the forced collectivization of agriculture and business, and 3) the persecution of the population by the SED party and the state security services. In 1959, 145.000 people left the GDR and East Berlin, about 91.000 via West Berlin; in 1960 the figure rose to almost 200.000 refugees, about 150.000 of whom fled via West Berlin.

The tense situation created by the currency reform, the Soviet blockade of West Berlin and the Western allied airlift in 1949-49, and the June 17, 1953 events was sharpened in the Fall of 1958 by another Berlin crisis as a result of Khrushchev's ultimatum aiming at transforming West Berlin into an "independent political entity." In sharply-worded separate notes each of the Western allies rejected the Soviet intention to abrogate the Four-Power Agreement on Berlin. The Soviet Union then abandoned the demands it had formulated in the form of an ultimatum, but threatened to sign a separate peace with the GDR. In this connection, the government and party leadership in the GDR, headed by Walter Ulbricht, hoped to finally close the still-open border with West Berlin, because the economic situation in the GDR was worsening from one month to the next due to the continually increasing wave of refugees leaving the country.

When, on June 15, 1961, Walter Ulbricht, speaking at a press conference in the Ministerial Building in Leipziger Straße, answered a question from a female correspondent representing the "Frankfurter Rundschau" with the tell-tale words: "No one intends to build a wall!" the boss of the SED party had in fact long since made up his mind to close the border to West Berlin, quite precisely with a wall. At the high point of the wave of refugees – before the building of the wall in the summer of 1961, 155,000 people had left the GDR and East Berlin in the first six months of the year – armed units of the GDR border police and members of the works combat units (paramilitary units organized by the nationalized companies and services) began erecting barbed wire barricades to seal off the border with West Berlin.

In the first twelve months, surveillance and control of the West Berlin border was the responsibility of the first and second border brigades of the riot police, which answered directly to the GDR minister for domestic affairs. The first brigade, under the command of Colonel Gerhard Tschitschke, was responsible for the border between East and West Berlin, while the second border brigade was commanded by Colonel Edwin Maseberg and was responsible for the border between the GDR and West Berlin. From the end of August, 1962, the two Berlin units of the border police were transferred to the Ministry for National Defense. This transfer had already been effected for the border brigades on the GDR-FRG border on September 15, 1961.

Up until the construction of the Berlin Wall, some 53.000 inhabitants of East Berlin and the neighboring region of the GDR had been working in West Berlin. From one day to the next, they lost their jobs. Things were much the same for around 13.000 West Berliners who worked in East Berlin – most of them also lost their jobs following the construction of the Berlin Wall. In addition, with the closing of the border regular commuter train and subway traffic between the two halves of the city came to a halt. Of the 81 remaining streets linking East and West Berlin, 67 were closed on August 13, 1961, and checkpoints were to be put up in the other 14. Up to the late afternoon of August 14, 1961, another 6.900 people managed to flee East Berlin and the DDR by crossing the still rudimentary wall.

Initially composed of fencing and barbed wire barricades, in the following months and years the Berlin Wall was continually enlarged and enhanced. It finally grew into a massive system that included a 13-foot-high concrete slab wall (termed the "fourth generation wall" in the professional literature), a lighting system, a 40-yard wide death strip (which the GDR border troops referred to as the action or control strip), a second wall facing East Berlin or Brandenburg, watch towers, trip-alarm fences, dog runs for patrol dogs, and sharpshooter positions.

The border zone was subject to special legal restrictions. East Berliners – including those who lived in the border zone – could only it with a special visa in their identity papers or with a special pass. The Berlin Wall system, which in the last years of its existence was almost 100 years wide – was only interrupted by seven crossing points after August 23, 1961. At first, practically only people from West Berlin and the FRG could use the crossing points, and this in the framework of rare travel pass agreements. For many long years after 1964, only retired East Berliners could cross the checkpoints to visit the West – and that only once a year.

Despite the barbed wire and the wall along the border to West Berlin and the border with West Germany, some 475.000 people managed to escape to the West between 1961 and 1989. In the same period, according to the latest official statistics, more than 125 people died at the Berlin Wall alone. The victims include a five-year-old Turkish boy, Cetin Mert, who drowned at the Gröbenufer on May 11, 1975, because GDR border troops prevented West Berlin policemen from coming to the rescue of the lad, who had fallen into the Spree River. One of the last victims was 20-year-old Chris Gueffroy, who was shot to death by GDR border guards on the night of February 6, 1989 while attempting to escape across the border between Treptow and Neukölln.

The first détente and improvement in relations between the two Germanies, and consequently between West Berlin and the GDR, came in 1971-72. Simultaneously with the Four-Power talks, talks were held between the GDR and the FRG, which led to agreements on basic principles, transit and circulation. Tourist traffic from the West to the East increased four-fold thanks to a simplified application procedure. Access to the Steinstuecken exclave was made possible through an exchange of territory with the GDR. For the first time since 1952, it became possible to phone from one side of the divided city to the other. As a result of the agreements, the two Germanies set up "permanent representations" in one another's territory.

Under the influence of Soviet General Secretary Mikhail Gorbachev's perestroika policy, domestic political problems sharpened in the 1980s and a growing opposition movement developed. Beginning in August 1989, large numbers of GDR citizens occupied the FRG embassies in Warsaw and Prague and the permanent representation in East Berlin. The Hungarian government allowed people to cross the Iron Curtain into Austria, and at practically the same time a peaceful revolution occurred in the GDR itself. These developments led to the fall of the Berlin Wall on November 9, 1989. Unfortunately, it was almost entirely torn down in the following months, and today practically no significant remnant of this inhuman structure remains within the city, which might serve as a memorial. In a short speech on the evening of November 10, 1989, former FRG chancellor Willy Brandt spoke in favor of keeping "a piece of this abominable construction standing … as a memorial to a historic monstrosity." But today only six small fragments of the Berlin Wall remain, as for example near the memorial in Bernauer Straße, which only communicate in an unsatisfactory way the terror of the GDR border policy and the reasons for the construction of the Berlin Wall.

Brandenburg Gate

The construction of the Berlin Wall on August 13, 1961 added a new date to the row of historic events in which the Brandenburg Gate was the focal point of German history. The monument in the classical style remained a city gate for one more day – it was initially intended to be used as one of the border crossing points – before it became, on August 14 and for many years thereafter, an inaccessible structure in the middle of the no man's land between East and West. Indeed, following the spontaneous protests staged by hundreds of West Berliners at the historically-charged Brandenburg Gate, the GDR party and government leaders feared further uncontrollable "acts of provocation" and struck the Brandenburg gate from the list of border crossing points one day later. Those same manifestation of discontent on the part of West Berliners led the British occupation authority – whose occupation zone bordered the Brandenburg Gate – to put up barbed wire barricades along the border line in the square fronting the Brandenburg Gate (today the Square of March 18) in order to prevent the people of West Berlin from engaging in ill-considered protest actions.

In the night of August 12-13, at about 1:05 in the morning, all the lights at the Brandenburg Gate suddenly went out. In the dark, GDR border police units and members of the works combat units appeared and began sealing off the through street, which until then had been open in both directions, and the surrounding area as well. The West Berlin police observing the scene briefly thought that the GDR was about to invade West Berlin, but were soon able to determine that the GDR military units stopped exactly on the border line.

In the following years, the Brandenburg Gate became the definitive symbol for the divided city. Both sides exploited the spot. The Berlin Senate and the GDR regime invited their respective guests and foreign delegations to climb onto specially-erected observation platforms and take a look over the wall into the other half of the city, representing the opposing social system. Nevertheless, the words spoken by U.S. President Ronald Reagan at the Brandenburg Gate on July 12, 1987, remain unforgettable: "Mr. Gorbachev, tear down this wall!" At the time, no one thought it possible that, just two and a half years later, the wall would no longer exist.

Works combat units and border police armored personnel carriers at the Brandenburg Gate in the night of August 13, 1961 11:00 p.m.

The first provisional barriers on Ebertstraße the day after the borders closed – 13th of August 1961, 12:00.

Border police armored personnel carriers in the square in front of the Brandenburg Gate – 14th of August 1961.

Building the "second generation" wall at the Brandenburg Gate –
20th November 1961.

Erection of the permanent "second generation" wall in front of the
Brandenburg Gate, in the foreground fences screen the building
work – 20th November 1961.

Barbed wire fence erected by British allies and West Berlin policemen at the Brandenburg Gate to prevent the people of West Berlin from staging ill-considered protests against the building of the Berlin Wall by the GDR – 31th October 1961.

Potsdamer Platz

In the decades preceding the Berlin Wall, the Potsdamer Platz had been a world-famous center of finance and business, the throbbing hub of urban traffic. It consequently was particularly hard hit by the construction of the wall. The square had already suffered severe damage during World War II. Its slow destruction continued with the razing of the Columbus building after the June 17, 1953 uprising. The border between the American, British and Soviet sectors met almost exactly in the middle of the square. Large portions that were in the Soviet sector were swallowed up in the months after August 13, 1961 by the sophisticated architecture of the Berlin Wall, with its ample death strip. The GDR tore down more and more buildings in the months following August 13.

Within the framework of a 1972 exchange of territory between the East and West, West Berlin obtained the barren tract of land formerly occupied by the Potsdamer train station and the ruins of the neighboring Vaterland building. The West Berlin authorities consigned the once-world famous building to the wrecker's ball. On the West Berlin side, only the Weinhaus Ruth and what remained of the Esplanade Hotel, between Bellevuestraße and the Potsdamer Platz, were spared from urban renewal. After re-unification, the Esplanade Hotel was included in the renovation of the Potsdamer Platz.

A never-ending stream of tourists came to the observation platform on the West Berlin side because a visit to the Potsdamer Platz was a must on the itinerary of practically every tour of West Berlin. From the platform, they could look down on the bare expanse of the empty square, which in fact had been turned into one gigantic death strip. They could also observe the continual improvements the GDR border troops made to the wall complex, which included not only the wall, but also barbed wire, death strips, anti-tank obstacles and anti-vehicle trenches.

Despite the enormous size of the unreal no man's land, the old magic of the historically-charged square must still have been working in November 1989. A mere three days after the fall of the Berlin Wall, on November 12, GDR border troops opened a crossing point at the Potsdamer Platz. Within a very short space of time, the throbbing life of the city had reconquered the former wasteland.

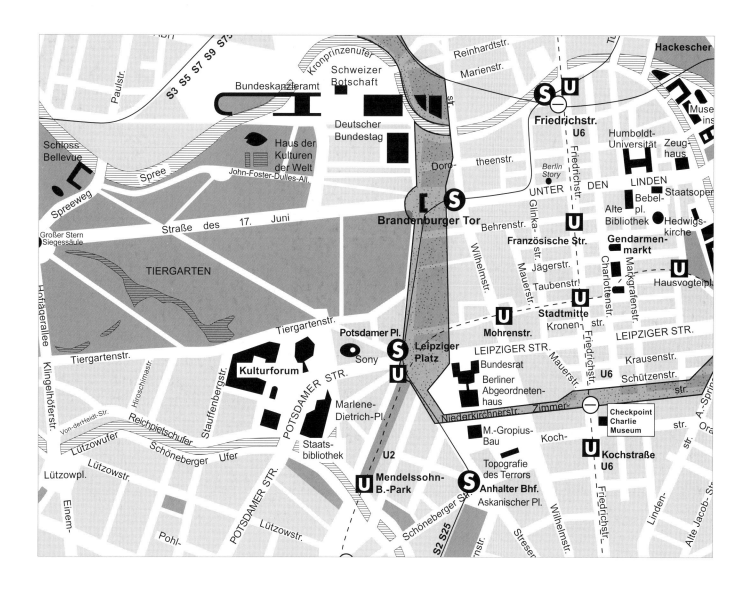

East German border police putting up the first barbed wire fence – 14th August 1961.

The "first generation" Berlin Wall scrupulously followed the line separating the border between the Berlin city wards and the occupation sectors – October 1961.

Reinforcement of the Berlin Wall with camouflage nets, anti-tank obstacles and widening of the death strip, in the background Strese-mannstraße, to the right, the ruins of the "Vaterland" building – 20th November 1961.

West Berlin police watch post at the wall at Potsdamer Square – 3rd September 1964.

West Berliners drinking coffee in front of the Berlin Wall at Pots-
damer Square – 24th August 1961.

Selling souvenirs at Potsdamer Square, in the background, the
visitors viewing platform – August 1972.

The "third generation" Berlin Wall with a cylindrical top, which stopped refugees from getting a handhold and climbing over –
23rd September 1966.

The splitting up of families and friends

From one day to the next, the Berlin Wall divided entire families, separated friends, and of course sundered lovers. It completely cut apart a throbbing city. Before the wall was built, hundreds of thousands of Berliners and people living in the suburbs in Brandenburg had crossed the border daily – often several times in a day – in order to work on the other side, to visit friends and relatives, to go shopping, to go to the cinema or the theater, to go swimming at the beach in Wannsee, or to amuse themselves in other ways.

On August 23, 1961, the last border crossing open to West Berliners was closed. From that day on, the GDR demanded that the West Berliners show travel passes, which they were to apply for at the Zoologischer Garten train station. But the West Berlin Senate refused to give its approval, and the arrangement could not come into force. The Deutsche Reichsbahn was responsible for the commuter train stations and the rail network on West Berlin soil, and they were consequently legally a part of the GDR. From that day on, East and West Berliners were separated for a long time. In the beginning, people could still wave to one another. Later, the GDR border police added screens to the barbed wire barricades to prevent this. Not until the West Berlin Senate and the GDR negotiated an agreement on travel passes in December 1963 was it possible for West Berliners to visit their relatives in East Berlin, between December 20 1963 and January 5, 1964. This first opportunity in two and a half years was used by around 730.000 West Berliners to make 1.2 million visits to relatives in the other half of the city.

Before the building of the Berlin Wall, around 53.000 people from East Berlin and the surrounding area of Brandenburg worked in West Berlin, while around 13.000 West Berliners worked in the Eastern half of the city. Months before the construction of the wall, the GDR had begun a hysterical propaganda campaign against the East Berliners and the people in the surrounding GDR who worked in West Berlin. From August 4, 1961, these people had to register, according to orders from the GDR authorities. The consequence of this measure was another jump in the number of refugees. After August 13, people who had been working in West Berlin had to report to their last job they had held in East Berlin, or else had to find a new job. Given the labor shortage in the socialist economy, in most cases that was not a problem. The West Berliners who had been working in East Berlin – most of whom were rail workers employed by the Deutsche Reichsbahn, doctors and other medical personnel working in the hospitals, or again artists appearing on the stage in East Berlin – also lost their jobs soon after the building of the Berlin Wall. In retaliation for the sealing off of the borders by the GDR party and government leaders, the West Berlin police stopped many West Berliners who worked in the East German hospitals from going to work in the days following August 23, 1961. The goal was to further destabilize the already-precarious provision of health care in the GDR.

The wall separates friends at Lohmühlenbrücke. The girls in the foreground and the two GDR border police are in Lohmühlenplatz in the Soviet sector, while the young men are in the American sector. In the background, the transformer substation at Paul-Lincke-Ufer in Kreuzberg, in the American sector – 15th August 1961.

Two girlfriends talking over the "first generation" wall at Harzer Straße on the sector border – 23rd August 1961.

A wedding couple and marriage guests on the Bernauer Straße sidewalk in the French sector of West Berlin wave to family members on the second floor of a building in the Soviet sector – 8th September 1961.

West Berliners waving to family and friends in the East Berlin at the sector border at the corner of Bernauer and Brunnenstraße – 24th August 1961.

Passing goods from West Berlin sidewalk to the neighbor lady in East Berlin at the corner of Brunnen- and Bernauer Straße – 8th September 1961.

A woman in Brunnenstraße in West Berlin waves to relatives in East Berlin over the temporary provisional wall – 23rd August 1961.

The forced evacuation of apartment buildings along the border

A short while after the closing of the borders and the beginning of construction of a wall in the heart of the city, the GDR began the forced evacuation of apartment buildings in the forbidden zone so as to close the window of opportunity for further escape and "to free up open space for observation and for shooting." After walling up the building entrances and the windows facing West Berlin, the next measure taken by the GDR regime, after August 21, 1961, was the forced evacuation of buildings along the border. Almost 2.000 people had to pack up their furniture and leave their homes in just one such action, in the Bernauer Strasse on September 24, 1961. Over a distance of almost a mile – from the Schwedter Straße to the Gartenstraße – 37 shops, 50 building entrances and 1.235 windows were walled up. Stumbling blocks and barbed wire obstacles were set up on the roofs t make it impossible to escape that way.

In the following years, in particular, the GDR leadership carried out extensive relocation and demolition work. Entire stretches of streets, apartment buildings, workshops and cemeteries were torn down and cleared away to make room for the establishment of the notorious death strips – which were initially termed action strips and later control strips in GDR jargon. In addition to the total destruction of portions of cemeteries, whose tombs were removed or leveled, entire cemeteries that lay directly on the East Berlin side of the border were declared to be in the forbidden zone. This was the case in Scharnhorst-, Liesen- and Bernauer Straße. Only people who had a pass could go to visit the graves of family members – and that only at specified times. In many places, dog runs for guard dogs were set up straight across cemeteries in the forbidden zone, to make it more difficult for people to escape across a terrain that was difficult to keep under surveillance.

Forced emptying of houses at the border in Bernauer Straße in the Mitte district – 24th September 1961.

One of the first things that the GDR border police did at buildings facing the West Berlin border was to wall up the front entrances and to close off the ground floor windows with barbed wire, as here in Bernauer Straße – 4th September 1961.

The forced evacuation of buildings on the border under the watchful eye of the border brigade of the riot police. Two policemen it difficult for the photographer in West Berlin to take photos – 1st October 1961.

An apartment building on the border between Mitte and Wedding, at the corner of Bernauer and Wolliner Straße, is blown up 1967.

Clearing of the allotment gardens in Klemkestraße, which the small allotment holders had been forced to abandon. Construction of the Berlin Wall with barbed wire fence and death strip – 26th September 1961.

Escaping across the Berlin Wall

About 1.6 million people from East Berlin and the GDR had abandoned their homes and escaped over the still relatively-open border to West Berlin before the Berlin Wall was built on August 13, 1961. Now, after the access routes to West Berlin had been closed, the number of refugees dropped but the flow of refugees did not come to a complete halt. Many East Berliners escaped, taking advantage of the fact that the obstacles that lay in their way were still relatively easy to overcome. They leapt from the windows of buildings facing on the border, swam across the streams and lakes, or climbed over the not yet very high and not always well-guarded walls and fences.

The East Berlin police president's office kept very precise statistics on the "border penetrations" (as they were termed in GDR jargon) that were observed by the police or reported to them. Thus it chalked down, for the second half of August, 1961, and just on the border between East and West Berlin, 100 cases involving the flight of 158 persons to West Berlin. Separate statistics were kept on desertions by members of the East Berlin police. In the same period, the political department chalked down 56 cases of members of the people's police and the riot police crossing over the border between

East and West Berlin. Incomplete official statistics indicate that about 300 members of the GDR border police had deserted by the end of 1961. Among the ways of escaping undetected, there was for example the one consisting in using doctored identity papers and foreign passports. A spontaneous effort by Westerners made it possible for many East Berliners to escape in this way shortly after the erection of the Berlin Wall. In all, the West Berlin refugee camp in Marienfelde tallied 25.403 refugees from East Berlin and the GDR in the period from August 13 to December 31, 1961.

On the early evening of May 23, 1962, GDR border troops opened fire on a 15-year-old boy who was trying to swim across the Schiffahrtskanal to West Berlin, in the vicinity of the Sandkrugbruecke. After demanding that they cease fire without obtaining any result, West Berlin police began shooting to cover the boy's escape. Peter Goehring, the non-commissioned officer commanding the GDR border troops, was shot dead.

Many West Berliners did not content themselves with protest actions against the wall in the period immediately following its construction. Instead, they attempted to actively assist those attempting to escape. One of them, Harry Seidel – who himself fled from East to West Berlin on August

13, 1961, and who was a member of an escape assistance organization – was arrested by GDR border guards on November 14, 1962, while piercing a tunnel between the Zehlendorf district and the Kleinmachnow district. In a show trial, the highest GDR court condemned him on December 29, 1962 to life at hard labor for "aggravated violation of the law on the maintenance of peace." In 1966, the FRG succeeded in buying Seidel's freedom.

East Berlin public transport police retrieve the body of Günter Litfin from the Humboldt-Hafen. Litfin was the first refugee to be shot at the Berlin Wall – 24th August 1961.

A family escapes through the ground floor window of an apart-ment building in West Berlin to the sidewalk in Bernauer Straße – 17th August 1961.

Harry Seidel's wife and friends protest at the Berlin Wall in Sebastianstraße in Kreuzberg district against his imprisonment in the GDR. Seidel was captured while helping East Berliners to escape – 13rd April 1963.

One family managed to escape across border point Drewitz in this bus, equipped with steel plates and a snowplow. The photo was taken at the Marienfelde emergency refugee camp – 26th Dezember 1962.

GDR border troops fill in an escape tunnel in Bernauer Straße, which was discovered before it could be used – 25th February 1971.

Memorials to victims of the Berlin Wall

In the first weeks and months following August 13, 1961, there were repeated attempts to flee by crossing the not yet unconquerable border to West Berlin. The escape attempts in what were termed the border streets along the border in the center of the city, such as the Bernauer Straße, the Harzer Straße and the Heidelberger Straße, were particularly spectacular because they often took place in broad daylight and under the very eyes of passersby. This was also where the first deaths occurred, such as those of Ida Siekmann and Rudolf Urban, who mortally injured themselves jumping from the upper floors of East German apartment buildings down to the sidewalk in West Berlin. The West Berliners spontaneously put up crosses and memorials dedicated to the memory of these victims. In the following years, the dead were remembered with wreath-laying ceremonies at these memorials.

On August 24, 1961, a 24-year-old tailor named Günter Litfin tried to reach West Berlin by swimming across the Humboldt Hafen. GDR public transport police spotted him and ordered him to halt. Situation report number 534, made at 4:50 p.m. on August 24, 1961 to the office of the president of the people's police in East Berlin states bluntly: "When challenged, the individual leapt into the Spree River and attempted to swim to West Berlin. A member of the public transport police fired warning shots with his submachine gun, but the individual paid no heed. As the individual swam on, the guard took aim and fired, and the individual sank beneath the water. The waterway police inspectorate has begun a search." Thus Günter Litfin, whose body was recovered from the Spree at around 7:10 p.m. and taken to the people's police hospital, became the first refugee to be shot at the Berlin Wall by East Berlin border police who were shooting with intent to kill.

But it was another death at the Berlin Wall that particularly upset not only the people of Berlin, but the whole Western world, and which came to be engraved in people's minds as representative of the wall's victims. This was the attempted flight of an 18-year-old mason named Peter Fechter. Together with a workmate, he attempted to escape in Zimmerstraße, not far from Checkpoint Charlie, on August 17, 1962, that is, about a year after the wall was put up. Actually, they had already gotten through all of the obstacles when GDR border guards began shooting at them. Fechter's friend managed to clamber over the last wall, but Fechter was hit by several bullets and lay seriously wounded on the eastern side of the wall. He bled to death, calling out for help, under the eyes and within earshot of hundreds of Berliners on both sides of the wall. Help could not reach him from the West, and the GDR border troops only came to his assistance after 50 minutes. Peter Fechter's painful, almost hour-long struggle with death clearly illustrated the horror of the Berlin Wall to the entire world.

Memorial cross and flower wreaths for Peter Fechter at the corner of Markgrafen- and Zimmerstraße, Fechter bled to death behind the wall after being shot while trying to climb the wall – 20th August 1962.

Memorial to Ida Siekmann, who was fatally injured on August 22, 1961 when she leapt from the third-floor window of her apartment at number 48, Bernauer Straße to the sidewalk in West Berlin.

Silent vigil at Friedrich-List-Ufer for Günter Litfin, who was shot by GDR public transport police on August 24, 1961, as he swam across the Humboldt-Hafen from East to West Berlin – 5th October 1962.

Memorial cross to Heinz Schöneberger at the Heinrich-Heine-Straße border crossing. Schöneberger, from Dortmund, who was shot by GDR border troops as he rammed his way across the border in a car carrying two women. Seriously wounded, he managed to reach West Berlin but dies shortly after – July 1968.

Memorial and cross to the memory of the first victim of the Berlin Wall, 47-year-old Rudolf Urban. Together with other inhabitants of the building, Urban was rappelling down the wall from the window of his apartment in Bernauer Straße on August 19, 1961, when he fell. He died of his injuries on September 17, 1961 – May 1977.

The border at Reinickendorf

The Berlin Wall, or better, the Berlin Wall complex, was almost as oppressive in the open countryside, running through meadows and fields, as it was in the Bernauer Straße or the Heidelberger Straße. In the open country it was almost more unreal and inappropriate than in the city amid rows of buildings and other walls.

About one third of the Reinickendorf district bordered on the neighboring Pankow district to the east, and a good two-thirds of it bordered on the GDR to the north and west. The northern-most stretch of the border within the city stretched from the city limits to Brandenburg, from the Tegel stream past the grounds of the former socialist company Bergmann-Borsig along the commuter train tracks to the Wollankstraße train station. Then the wall complex cut across the open, in part cultivated area before running along the old Niederbarnim railroad line and the Märkisches Viertel down the western side to the urbanized neighborhoods of Pankow and Reinickendorf. In the middle of the fields and fallow land the wall complex was laid out over a considerably wide stretch right from the very beginning, so as to make escape impossible. To complete the picture, there was the spooky way the border strip and the barbed wire barricades were lit up every night. The whole thing made one think of a prison camp.

On the West Berlin side, excursion ships cruised from the Tegel harbor out on Lake Tegel and on the Havel River. During their voyages, the helmsmen on the excursion steamers had to follow the prescribed route exactly, as the border between East and West, which they durst not cross, ran roughly through the middle of the Havel.

Floodlights on the old freight train tracks along the sector border between Lübars and Rosenthal – March 1966.

Protected by French sentinels, West Berlin police clear the rubble of the Berlin Wall, which collapsed in the night along the border in Klemke-straße. In the background, East Berlin border guards – 31st March 1962.

The Berlin Wall at the Wittelsruh commuter train station, which is in West Berlin. Behind the wall, a propaganda poster put up by the Studios at the Barbed Wire, financed by the West Berlin Senate. The poster reads: "We know you don't want to destroy togetherness" – 6th June 1966.

The border, sealed off with barbed wire fences, the death strip, observation bunkers, guard towers, patrol road and floodlights in the Blank-enfelder Chaussee area by Lübars – July 1969.

The border, sealed off with a barbed wire fence and the "third gene-ration" wall at Blankenfelder Chaussee near Lübars. In the back-ground, two DDR border troop watch towers, a new concrete one and an old wooden one – July 1969.

The "third generation" wall with death strip, patrol road, observa-tion bunker, anti-tank obstacles, floodlight pylons, and trip-alarm fence on Quickborner Straße, in the background Friedrich-Engels-Straße in East Berlin – May 1976.

The West Berlin ship "Moby Dick" on Nieder-Neuendorf lake in front of the road in Heiligensee. In the background, the wall and watch towers on the outskirts of Nieder-Neuendorf in the GDR. The border between East and West ran almost directly though the middle of the lake – June 1980.

The Berlin Wall between the Mitte and Wedding districts

Bernauer Straße was one of the most horrible sections of the Berlin Wall in the city, during the period when Berlin was divided. The border ran the whole length of the street from the Schwedter Straße to the Gartenstraße. This corresponded to the old border line between the city districts of Mitte and Wedding. The facades on the southern side of the street belonged to the Soviet sector, whereas the southern sidewalk, the whole street and the northern sidewalk were all in the French sector of West Berlin. In the years before the city was divided, you paid for goods in Ost-Marks in the shops on the southern side of the street, whereas in the shops on the northern side you paid in D-Marks, the currency used in West Berlin.

Three days after August 13, the entrance doors to the apartment buildings on the East Berlin side of the street were locked shut, and beginning on August 18 the border police began bricking up the entrances. Since in the following weeks increasing numbers of East Berliners used these buildings, in particular the upper floors, for escape attempts, the GDR began in the Fall of 1961 the forced evacuation of Bernauer Straße and other streets where the border followed a similar line. In 1965, the buildings on the East Berlin side of the street were almost completely torn down. In many places, only the front facades of the ground floor were left standing and incorporated into the Berlin Wall complex. Finally, in 1979 they too were replaced with the concrete "fourth generation" wall.

The Church of Reconciliation stood on the East Berlin side of the Bernauer Straße. The majority of the parish, torn in two by the construction of the wall in 1961, lived in West Berlin. After August 13, 1961, the church could no longer be used as it lay right in the middle of the forbidden zone, and it was locked up. On October 23, 1961, the Church of Reconciliation parish meeting hall and the neighboring Burckhardt building, a Protestant institute for cultural, social and youth work, were both completely evacuated.

On the first Christmas after the building of the wall, Regine Radischewski, then a member of the parish – later, following her marriage, minister of Brandenburg Regine Hildebrandt – sent the Mitte district council a written request to put a lighted advent star up on the spire of the walled-up Church of Reconciliation. Her request was turned down by the East Berlin authorities, as was that of her future husband, the son of Rev. Helmut Hildebrandt, to be allowed to have the church bells rung on Christian holidays. Through the years, the church, standing just behind the Berlin Wall, but remaining inaccessible, became a special symbol of the divided city. The church became even more famous when GDR border troops blew the church buildings up in 1985. The images of the collapsing church tower were seen around the world.

Among the absurdities of the divided city one must also mention the Wollankstraße train station on the north-south commuter line. The station lay in the East Berlin district of Pankow, right on the border with the West Berlin district of Wedding. Only West Berliners could use it. A sign at the entrance to the train station nevertheless warned commuter train travelers with these words: "Warning! This entrance and the train station are in the Soviet sector."

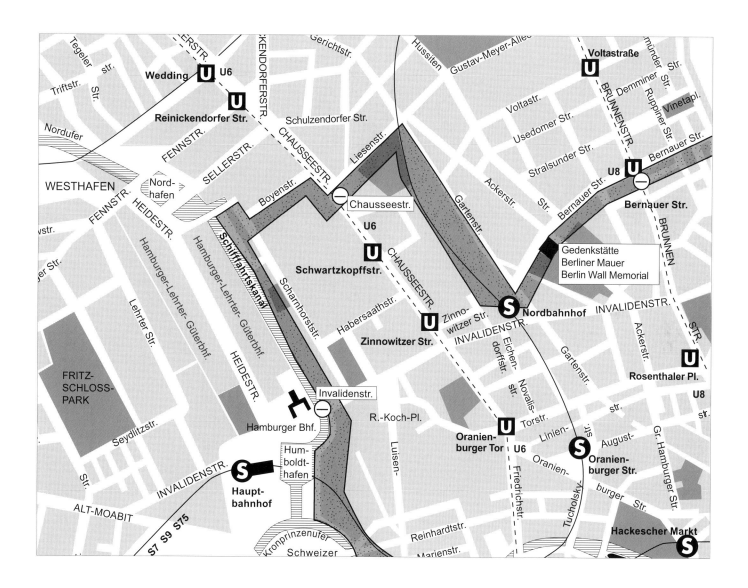

Tegeler **U** U6 Wedding

str.

Triftstr. Str.

U

Nordufer **U** Reinickendorfer Str.

WESTHAFEN

Nord-
hafen

FENNSTR.

HEIDESTR.

FENNSTR.

SELLERSTR.

KENDORFERSTR.

CHAUSSEESTR.

Gerichtstr.

Hussiten

Gustav-Meyer-Allee

U Voltastraße

münder Str.

Demminer Str.

Ruppiner Str.

Vinetapl.

BRUNNENSTR.

Schulzendorfer Str.

Boyenstr.

Liesenstr.

Voltastr.

Usedomer Str.

Stralsunder Str.

Ackerstr.

Str.

Bernauer Str.

Str.

Bernauer Str.

U U8 **U**

Bernauer Str.

BRUNNEN

U

Str.

Chausseestr.

U6

U Schwartzkopffstr.

Hamburger-Lehrter-Güterbhf.

Hamburger-Lehrter- Güterbhf.

Schiffffahrtskanal

Scharnhorststr.

CHAUSSEESTR.

Habersaathstr.

Gartenstr.

Gedenkstätte
Berliner Mauer
Berlin Wall Memorial

Zinno-
witzer Str.

S Nordbahnhof

INVALIDENSTR.

Lehrter Str.

Hamburger-

str.

U Zinnowitzer Str.

INVALIDENSTR.

Eichen-
dorffstr.

Novalis
str.

Gartenstr.

Ackerstr.

Str.

U Rosenthaler Pl.

U8

str.

FRITZ-
SCHLOSS-
PARK

HEIDESTR.

Invalidenstr.

R.-Koch-Pl.

Torstr.

Linien-

str.

Aug ust-

Gr. Hamburger Str.

Seydlitzstr.

Hamburger Bhf.

Humboldt-
hafen

Luisen-

U Oranien-
burger Tor

U6

Friedrichstr.

Oranien-

str.

S Oranien-
burger Str.

burger Str.

Str.

INVALIDENSTR.

S Haupt-
bahnhof

ALT-MOABIT

S7 S9 S75

Kronprinzenufer

Schweizer

Reinhardtstr.

Marienstr.

Tucholsky-

str.

Hackescher Markt

S

The "first generation" wall, screened off by a fence facing the West Berlin side at the corner of Bernauer and Schwedter Straße. The bricked-up house on the right is in East Berlin, Oderberger Straße is on the left – 21st November 1961.

Bricked-up houses that had been forcibly evacuated on the East Berlin side of Bernauer Straße, while the rest of the street including both side-walks is in West Berlin. The West Berlin streetcar continued to run down the street in the first years after the building of the wall – 20th March 1962.

Reinforcement of the "first generation" wall. Top left in the picture, the corner of Boyen- and Chausseestraße in the Wedding district in West Berlin – 17th July 1962.

Sealing off West Berlin at the sector border on the corner of the Bernauer- and Strelitzer Straße. The GDR border police are keeping an eye on a crowd of East Berliners – 14th August 1961.

This is what you could see from the viewing platform at the corner of Schwedter and Bernauer Straße, behind the facades of the torn-down ground floor buildings, the "fourth generation" wall, which has been reinforced with a control (death) strip and a trip-alarm fence – 16th April 1980.

The nave of the Church of Reconciliation has already been demolished. DDR border troops will blow up the church tower in early 1985 –
28th January 1985.

The Berlin Wall between Mitte and Kreuzberg

The construction of the wall had serious consequences for both city districts, for both Mitte in East Berlin and for Kreuzberg in West Berlin. The Mitte district was home to almost all of the important East Berlin government and party headquarters. However, it was surrounded on three sides – to the north, west and south – by what might be called "enemy territory." This was one of the reasons why many East Berliners had the impression that they were walled in. The same thing went for the SO 36 sector of Kreuzberg which – formerly a part of downtown Berlin – was turned by the events of August 13, 1961 into an urban dead end. In the course of the following years, this nurtured the development of a variety of counter-cultures.

Because the border at the intersection of Zimmerstraße and Lindenstraße made a sudden turn to the northeast, it was possible for photographer Horst Siegmann to photograph the construction workers and their guards in East Berlin from behind. Five years later, just a little to the west of this spot, Axel Springer built a highrise building for his publishing house right up against the Berlin Wall, as a symbol of the free Western world. As can be seen on one of the photographs in this section, "Albertzlauben" served as a bulletproof shelter and observation post for the West Berlin police. They were named after the West Berlin Senator of the time – later the mayor of West Berlin – Heinrich Albertz, during whose term these shelters were put up.

In the old Luisenstadt district, which was split up in 1920 between the newly-created districts of Mitte and Kreuzberg, the border between the Soviet and American sectors followed the characteristic curve laid out by Peter Joseph Linne, when he built the Luisenstaedtische canal to link the Spree River and the Engel basin. (The canal was filled in in the 1920s.)

It was also in this area that the border along the Leuschnerdamm and the Bethaniendamm lay directly on the southern row of apartment buildings. The southern row of houses belonged to the American sector, whereas the sidewalk in front and the whole street belonged to the Soviet sector. However, as was often the case in this kind of situation, the GDR erected the Berlin Wall on the East Berlin side, a few yards away from the exact boundary line. As a result, these zones in West Berlin took on an air of narrow old city-center lanes, of the kind that can only be seen in prints of medieval city scenes. The East Berlin side walk and

The bit of street, as for example in the Sebastianstraße, could be walked down and driven on by West Berliners. In the case of an accident or a violation of the law, however, the West Berlin police could not intervene. Only the allied military police had that right in these little sections of East Berlin.

The Berlin Wall in Kreuzberg, and in particular the above-mentioned curved section, became very popular with both known and unknown artists once the GDR border soldiers had erected the whitewashed "fourth generation" concrete wall. On the West Berlin side, the wall became a large-format "canvas" for painted and spray-painted artwork.

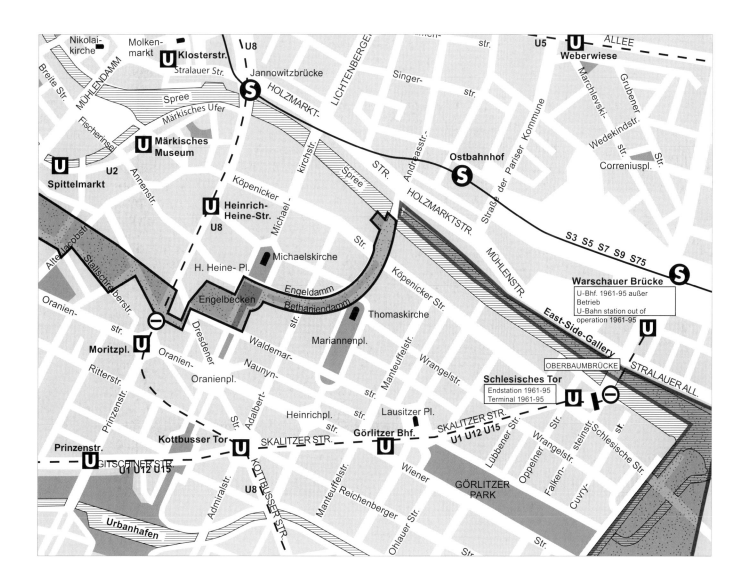

Nikolai-
kirche

Molken-
markt

U **Klosterstr.**

U8

Stralauer Str.

S Jannowitzbrücke

HOLZMARKT.

Breite Str.

MÜHLENDAMM

Spree

Märkisches Ufer

Fischerinsel

U **Märkisches
Museum**

Köpenicker

U2

U

Spittelmarkt

Annenstr.

kirchstr.

Spree

STR.

Michael -

U5 **U**
Weberwiese

ALLEE

Marchlevski-

Grubener

str.

Wedekindstr.

str.

Correniuspl.

Ostbahnhof

S

HOLZMARKTSTR.

Straße der Pariser Kommune

S3 S5 S7 S9 S75

MÜHLENSTR.

S

U **Heinrich-
Heine-Str.**

U8

Str.

Michaelskirche

Köpenicker Str.

Alte Jacobstr.

Stallschreiberstr.

H. Heine- Pl.

Engeldamm

Engelbecken

Bethaniendamm

Thomaskirche

Warschauer Brücke
U-Bhf. 1961-95 außer
Betrieb
U-Bahn station out of
operation 1961-95

East-Side-Gallery

U

Oranien-

str.

⊖

U

Moritzpl.

Dresdener

Oranien-

Waldemar-

Naunyn-

Oranienpl.

str.

Marianneapl.

Manteuffelstr.

Wrangelstr.

OBERBAUMBRÜCKE

STRALAUER ALL.

Schlesisches Tor
Endstation 1961-95
Terminal 1961-95

U **⊖**

Ritterstr.

Prinzenstr.

Adalbert-

Heinrichpl.

str.

Lausitzer Pl.

str.

SKALITZER STR.

Str.

Schlesische Str.

Prinzenstr.

U

GITSCHINER STR.

Kottbusser Tor

U

SKALITZER STR.

Görlitzer Bhf.

U

U1 U12 U15

Lübbener Str.

Str.

Wrangelstr.

Oppelner Str.

steinstr.

U1 U12 U15

KOTTBUSSER STR.

U8

Admiralstr.

Manteuffelstr.

Reichenberger

Wiener

**GÖRLITZER
PARK**

Falken-

Cuvry-

Urbanhafen

Ohlauer Str.

Str.

Str.

65

Reinforcement of the wall and erection of tank traps in front of the building housing DDR ministries on Niederkirchnerstraße. The sign reads: "Whoever attacks us will be annihilated" – 20th November 1961.

A look down Wilhelmstraße with the "first generation" wall. In the left background the building housing the ministries on the East Berlin side – 23rd August 1961.

Building of the first cinderblock wall on the sector border at the corner of Linden- and Zimmerstraße, in the foreground the East Berlin Mitte district – 18th August 1961.

The Berlin Wall at the corner of Waldemarstraße and Legiendamm. In the center of the picture, visibility blinds have been erected over the Luisen canal. In the background West Berlin apartment buildings on Leuschnerdamm – April 1962.

This photo shows the "first generation" wall, reinforced by the "second generation" wall of concrete slabs laid one on top of the other, at the corner of Linden- and Zimmerstraße. On the left-hand, West Berlin side of the photo, an "Albertzlaube" shelter for the West Berlin police. The shelters were named after Senator Heinrich Albertz – 21st November 1961.

Reinforcing the Berlin Wall at the corner of Stresemann- and Niederkirchnerstraße – 28th July 1962.

The "third generation" Berlin Wall with death strip, trip-alarm fence, anti-tank obstacles and observation bunker at Bethaniendamm. On the right-hand side of the picture, the trade union building designed by Bruno and Max Taut (today ÖTV-Building) on Fritz-Heckert-Straße (Engeldamm) – February 1969.

The "first generation" wall at the corner of Sebastian- and Luckauer Straße. The apartment buildings on the left are in West Berlin, while the sidewalk is in East Berlin – 5th August 1968.

The "fourth generation' Berlin Wall on the corner of Sebastian- and Luckauer Straße. The apartment buildings are in West Berlin, but the sidewalk and the strip of street are in East Berlin – 1984.

Someone on the West Berlin side blew up part of the wall at the corner of Zimmer- and Charlottenstraße. A crowd of West Berliners looks through the hole in the wall – 28th July 1986.

US soldiers on patrol at the corner of Waldemar- and Luckauer Straße, following the escape of two GDR citizens –
25th September 1980.

Artist working on the Berlin Wall at Bethaniemdamm. St. Thomas Church can be seen in the background – September 1989.

The Berlin Wall between Treptow and Neukölln

Years before the construction of the Berlin Wall, the GDR used barriers and chain link fences to block off many of the little side streets running from the Eastern sector to the three Western sectors. Similarly, in sundry streets that formed the border between Treptow and Neukölln, the East Berlin works combat units initially put up chain link fences down the middle of the road. Weeks later, the East Berlin border police chopped down the trees lining the street, the better not only to see refugees, but also to shoot them.

The border between Neukölln and Treptow in the area of Bouchéstraße and Heidelberger Straße followed a similarly radical route to that in the Bernauer Straße, between the Mitte and Wedding districts. One row of buildings, the street, and both sidewalks lay in East Berlin, whereas the other row of buildings and the little front gardens were in West Berlin. Due to this particular situation, in various areas on the West Berlin side "detour paths" had been run through the front gardens even before the construction of the wall. In this way, the West Berliners, who feared being arrested and dragged off, did not need not use the East Berlin sidewalk.

There were repeated escapes in the days and weeks following August 13 along the Heidekampgraben, on the border between the Soviet and American sectors in the area of the Köllnische Heide commuter train station and the East Berlin district of Baumschulenweg, because the wall in this sector was still very rudimentary and also because it was not so closely watched.

The Neukölln district had a 15-and-a-half mile border with East Berlin and the GDR. Nine-and-three-quarter miles of that border were with the East Berlin city district of Treptow, and the remaining five-and-three-quarter miles were with the GDR regional district of Königs Wusterhausen. In the latter sector the Berlin Wall complex was particularly elaborate and many-leveled, as the photographs taken near Buckow and Rudow clearly show.

This is one of the many streets that had already been sealed off before August 13, at the Lohmühlenbrücke. The apartment buildings in the background are in the Lohmühlenstraße – 13th August 1961, 14:20.

The Berlin Wall: a concrete slab wall, a border strip, an observation tower und floodlights at the corner of Heidelberger and Treptower Straße, The view is down Heidelberger Straße – July 1969.

GDR border troops cut down trees in the street on the East Berlin side of Heidelberger Straße in order to make escape more difficult –
20th April 1963.

GDR border troops clear a ten-yard-wide strip at Heidekampgraben for the erection of the wall and the creation of a death strip –
30th September 1961.

Houses being torn down on the East Berlin side of Harzer Straße. In the foreground, the part of Harzer Straße that lay in West Berlin. In the background, the GDR watch tower at Lohmühlenbruecke – 26th September 1967.

The Berlin Wall: a "third generation" wall reinforced with a death strip, observation towers, floodlight pylons and anti-tank obstacles along the border at Buckow Rudow in the GDR district of Koenigs Wusterhausen. In the background, the West Berlin satellite city of Gropiusstadt – August 1975.

View over the wall from Massanterbrücke at Teltow canal -- observation tower, death strip and anti-tank obstacles, in the background, apartment buildings in the Johnannisthal area – August 1975.

Propaganda wars between East and West

Just six days after the border was closed the West Berlin Senate launched the "Studio at the Barbed Wire" and its political activities. Using large-format posters and batteries of loudspeakers, the West informed the people of East Berlin and especially addressed appeals to the GDR guards stationed on the border.

After August 25, 1961, loudspeakers were also set up on the East Berlin side, particularly at such strategic points as the Brandenburg Gate, Potsdamer Platz, and the border crossing points at the corner of Friedrichstraße and Zimmerstraße and in the Heinrich-Heine-Straße. The GDR used these loudspeakers to engage in sometimes ear-splitting word duels with the West. Large-format posters were also set up at the Berlin Wall on the East Berlin side in order to spread propaganda about the role of the "anti-fascist protective wall" as a defensive measure against "Western imperialism" to the people in West Berlin. They also served as a counter-weight to the posters put up by West Berlin organizations, such as the "August 13 collective." In 1962, in addition to the posters and sound broadcasts, the West Berlin side began using gigantic "zippers" (lighted news bulletin boards). For example, one zipper was put on the GSW headquarters building in Kochstraße, and another on the school building near Bornholmer Straße. In this way political news was flashed to East Berliners in a form that was legible at a great distance. Years before the Berlin Wall was built, a similar zipper had already been put up at the Potsdamer Platz, on which East Berliners could read Western press bulletins. The "Studio at the Barbed Wire" ceased its activity in the late 1960s.

West Berlin wanted poster for a GDR border policeman accused of having shot to death a refugee trying to cross the border –
4th September 1961.

Loudspeaker van and propaganda poster of the "Studios at the Barbed Wire," which the West Berlin Senate financed. The poster on Bornholmer Straße quotes Walter Ulbricht: "No one intends to build a wall" – 16th October 1961.

"Studios at the Barbed Wire" poster on the border at the corner of Boyen- and Chausseestraße. The poster reads: "It all depends on the second man" – 16th May 1967.

"Studios at the Barbed Wire" poster at the corner of Linden- and Zimmerstraße. The poster reads: "All Germans thank the honest soldier, only the SED thanks the marksman. Under the poster, a loudspeaker van – 15th September 1965.

GDR propaganda banner warning West Berlin mayor Willy Brandt not to get fresh – "we're good marksmen." The photo was taken at the wall in Wilhelmstraße, on the border between Mitte and Kreuzberg – 20th November 1961.

A row of loud speaker vans belonging to the "Studios at the Barbed Wire" at the wall at the corner of Stresemann- and Niederkirchnerstraße, in the foreground a sign in four languages with which the Americans underlined their responsibility for the entire city under the four-power agreement – 28th July 1962.

"Zipper" mounted on the side of the GSW headquarters building in Kochstraße in the Kreuzberg district of West Berlin. The message on the zipper reads: "It's time to put an end to the order to shoot [escaping refugees]" – December 1963.

West Berlin Senate propaganda poster in front of the wall at the corner of Elsen- and Heidelberger Straße in Neukölln. The poster reads: "Unity and Justice and Freedom," which is the motto of the FRG – October 1962.

East Berlin propaganda poster at the border on the corner of Schwedter- and Bernauer Straße, looking down Eberswalder Straße. The poster reads "Concentration camp architect Lübke, how long will you continue to lie?" – 13th May 1966.

At the corner of Linden- and Zimmerstraße, on the border between Kreuzberg and Mitte districts, a propaganda poster put up by the "Studios at the Barbed Wire" at the barbed-wire-crowned Berlin Wall. On the left under the poster, a shelter for the West Berlin police – 25th March 1966.

Border crossing points

Before the Berlin Wall was built, there were still 81 open streets by which Berliners could cross from east to west or vice versa, in addition to the subway and commuter rail lines. On August 13, 1961, 67 of those roads were closed and later walled up, as were the streets that had previously been closed with chain link fences. Of the remaining crossing points, the Brandenburg Gate was closed on the following day, August 14, followed by other crossing points that the GDR had initially intended to keep open in Kopenhagener Straße, Wollankstraße, Brunnenstraße, Puschkinallee, Elsenstraße and Rudower Straße. Of the crossing points within the city limits – which practically only West Berliners could use – there remained 1) the Friedrichstraße border crossing for foreigners, diplomats and military personnel; 2) the Bornholmer Straße and Heinrich-Heine-Straße crossing points, for citizens of the Federal Republic of Germany; and 3) four border crossings for West Berliners, in Chausseestraße, Invalidenstraße, and Sonnenallee, and a pedestrian crossing at Oberbaumbrücke. For those traveling by train, initially from the Federal Republic, and later from West Berlin or the GDR, the only place to cross the border was the train station in Friedrichstraße. To this end, a solid steel wall was installed to separate the platforms used for travel within East Berlin from travel to or from West Berlin.

Checkpoint Charlie was the allied control post at the border crossing at the corner of Friedrichstraße and Zimmerstraße. From 1961 to 1990 it was the only border crossing between East and West Berlin open to members of the Allied military forces, and also to foreigners and diplomats. In the years that Berlin was divided it became a favorite place for protests on the West Berlin side aimed at drawing attention to the oppressed inhabitants of the GDR and the prisoners in the GDR.

In the month of October, 1961 Checkpoint Charlie was the scene of a confrontation between the Western allies and the Soviet Union. On October 22, GDR border troops suddenly began trying to check the passports of Allied soldiers, which the latter refused to permit, citing Berlin's quadripartite status. The GDR border troops continued trying to check passports, and then on October 25 several US tanks took up positions on the West Berlin side of Checkpoint Charlie. The next day the situation escalated when Soviet tanks without national insignia took up positions on the East Berlin side. The showdown continued for about 48 hours, with the two heavily armed superpowers facing one another at point-blank range. Once the Soviets and Americans had tried to bluff one another for almost two long days, the Soviets withdrew their tanks on the morning of October 28, and soon after the U.S. tanks also withdrew. Once the mutual stand-down had been carried out, Western Allied soldiers were again allowed to cross freely and uncontrolled over to the Soviet sector.

US soldiers behind a sand bag barricade at the Checkpoint Charlie border crossing point in the Friedrichstraße – 4th December 1961.

Escalation on the issue of the sovereignty rights of the Western Allies: Soviet tanks, their insignia removed, at the border crossing in the Friedrichstraße – October 1961.

Escalation on the issue of the sovereignty rights of the Western Allies: US tanks at Checkpoint Charlie in Friedrichstraße – 28th October 1961.

US army tanks in position at Checkpoint Charlie on Friedrichstraße – October 1961.

The border crossing on Invalidenstraße. A Soviet delegation on its way to lay wreaths at the Soviet cenotaph in the Straße des 17. Juni –
7th November 1961.

The south platforms for trains to West Germany (platform A) and to West Berlin (platform B) in the Friedrichstraße train station. A steel wall seals them off from platform C, reserved for East Berlin commuter trains – 1982.

Families from West Berlin at the border crossing at Oberbaum-brücke, on their way to visit friends and family in East Berlin. The visits are allowed under an Easter pass agreement – 19th April 1965.

Border check point in Heerstraße. Until 1987, this was the border crossing for the passage through the GDR on old Route 5 to Hamburg in West Germany – 8th December 1987.

The border between West Berlin and neighboring Brandenburg

On the initiative of the four World War II allies, the border in the Berlin area was shifted several times. For example, West Staaken was exchanged for a 425-acre expanse in the Weinmeisterhöhe, the so-called "Seeburg salient." However, this resulted in the absurd splitting of the village of Staaken, with the geographically eastern part belonging to West Berlin and the geographically western part belonging to the GDR district of Potsdam. Since the new border ran along the Finkenkruger Weg and the Nennhauser Damm, GDR border troops proceeded to tear down various buildings standing on the western side of the road, such as the post office.

The situation created by the construction of the Berlin Wall was particularly insane in the Gutsstraße in Groß-Glienicke, where the border between East and West ran right through the middle of a farmyard. Within a few years, the portions of farm buildings standing on the GDR side had been torn down.

If you drive out on Osdorfer Straße 1, in the vicinity of the Berlin city limits near Lichterfelde Ost, you fill find a stone memorial dating from 2003 and a single remaining barn. They are all that remind the visitor of the existence of the village of Osdorf. In the 1960s, the village was sacrificed to the extension of the Berlin Wall fortifications, and in 1968 Soviet troops stationed in the barracks in Wünsdorf razed the whole village, except for the barn. It only survived because GDR border troops needed it.

The borders laid down by the Allies after World War II cut Berlin off from some areas that were under Berlin's administrative jurisdiction but which lay in Brandenburg. With the construction of the Berlin Wall, the exclaves of Steinstuecken, Erlengrund and Fichtewiesen, as well as the near-exclave of Eiskeller were cut off from the Zehlendorf and Spandau districts. Within the framework of the 1972 Four-Power Agreement on Berlin and the accords between the West Berlin Senate and the GDR government, a connecting road for automobiles was built between the Spandau district and Eiskeller. An exchange of territory between the GDR and West Berlin made possible the establishment of a normal connecting road from the Zehlendorf to the Steinstücken exclave. Normal – except for the fact that the road was bordered on either side by the Berlin Wall.

Border fence, barbed wire barricades and screens in Marienfelder Allee in Marienfelde to the GDR district of Zossen – October 1961.

The Berlin Wall on Fingenkruger Weg in the divided town of Staa-
ken, in the foreground two West Berlin policemen – 9th January 1962.

Schoolchildren harvest potatoes in the forbidden zone under the
watchful eye of the GDR border police. In 1968, Soviet soldiers
razed the village and domain of Osdorf on the Licherfelde Süd bor-
der – 5th October 1962.

A British soldier in an armored reconnaissance vehicle accompanies a schoolboy on his way to Spandau. After August 13, 1961, the GDR border police forbade the inhabitants of the near-exclave of Eiskeller from using the road – 24th August 1961.

The Berlin Wall goes through a farmyard in the Ritterfeld domain on Gutsstraße in Groß-Glienicker See. In the following years, border troops tore down the building on the GDR side (to the right of the wall) – May 1962.

The view from the main gate of Glienicke hunting pavillion in West Berlin. The Waldmüllerstraße in Klein-Glienicke (Potsdam District) is closed off by barbed wire – 6th May 1963.

The 1972 Four Powers agreement led to an exchange of territory between the GDR and West Berlin. This permitted the building of a normal road (lined on both sides by the Berlin Wall) linking Zehlendorf to the Steinstücken exclave. The picture shows the inauguration of the road – 30th August 1972.

Road, open only to Western military personnel, between the Eiskeller near-exclave and the Spandau municipal forest – 15th February 1972.

The Soviet Union and the United States of America exchange spies and dissidents on the Glienicker Bridge, on the border between Potsdam and West Berlin. In the center of the photograph, behind the car door, Soviet civil rights activist Anatoly Shcharanski, with US ambassador Richard Burt to his left – 11th of February 1986.

The border at the West Berlin exclave of Erlengrund south of Nieder-Neuendorf in the GDR. The Erlengrund exclave lies along the Havel river to the right of the border strip. It is reached by the road that runs through the control strip, between the observation towers and the walls. To the left, the forest area belonging to the GDR – 22nd October 1976.

The Berlin Wall between Zehlendorf and Kleinmachnow on the Benschallee by the Düppel train station. From the left: the approach wall, a barbed wire fence, the patrol road, floodlight pylons, a watch tower, an anti-vehicle trench, the death strip and the wall facing West Berlin – 1983.

Graffiti and artwork on the Berlin Wall

The Berlin Wall evolved over the years from a barbed wire fence to a cinderblock wall to a concrete slab wall, and finally, in the late 1970s, into the "fourth generation" wall. The final version was composed of pre-fabricated reinforced concrete segments in the form of an inverted T and capped with a cylindrical top. Whereas in the initial stages the West Berlin side of the wall only presented isolated hand-written graffitti, the advent of the anarchistic "Sponti" movement and the squats was accompanied by the "tattooing" and exuberant painting of the wall in vivid colors. The uninterrupted whitewashed wall – a monument to narrow-mindedness – exasperated and challenged poets, artists and graffiti artists. Over the years, the Berlin Wall became a kind of barometer mirroring the mood of the dissident Zeitgeist or spirit of the age. In addition, many of the messages immortalized on the wall bore witness to West Berliners' changing relationship with this urban monstrosity. At one point, someone spray painted these words on the Bethaniendamm section of the Berlin Wall in Kreuzberg: "What are you gawking at? Haven't you ever seen a wall before?" The message was doubtlessly intended for the never-ending stream of tourists from the Federal Republic of Germany and from foreign countries. Lev Nussberg, the founder of the nonconformist Muscovite "Movement Group," was the first artist to propose, from his New York home in 1982, that the Berlin Wall be transformed into a superb, miles-long art exhibition by having all the great artists from around the world do paintings on it. Two years later, the museum "Haus am Checkpoint Charlie" held a contest to come up with the best idea on the theme of "Overcoming the Wall by painting the Wall." They received 288 proposals from Germany and abroad. The jury awarded the first prize to the painter and illustrator Matthias Hohl-Stein, whose exit visa had only been approved by the GDR authorities a few short months before. The prize-winning work depicted a GDR border guard on horseback leaping the wall from East to West Berlin like a gold-medal-winning Olympic steeplechase athlete.

The GDR export company Limex began doing business in Berlin Wall paintings after the wall fell on November 9, 1989. It began selling portions of the Berlin Wall. Limex sold a 100-yard stretch of the wall with paintings by the Berlin artist Kiddy Citny to the New York Museum of Modern Art for $295,000. When Citny demanded a share of the sales price, Limex informed him that he should be happy not to have to answer charges of "damaging property, to wit, border installations."

Graffiti and paintings on the wall at Bethaniendamm in Kreuzberg, in the background St. Thomas church – October 1984.

Graffiti and paintings on the "fourth generation" wall in Niederkirchnerstraße. In the background the former Prussian diet, which became the seat of the Berlin legislature after reunification – October 1984.

Paintings on the "fourth generation" wall at Bethaniendamm in Kreuzberg – 1986.

The fall and demolition of the Berlin Wall

It was in an off-hand way that Günter Schabowski, a member of the Politburo and newly-named Central Committee Secretary for Public Information made his announcement on November 9, 1989. He was answering a question from a journalist for the Italian press agency ANSA regarding the new travel regulations that the Council of Ministers of the GDR had just adopted, according to which "applications for private trips could henceforth be made without meeting preconditions (a statement on the purpose of the trip and a declaration concerning family relationships." Moreover, "free passage … by way of all border transit points from the GDR to the FRG and to West Berlin" was to be allowed.

When I heard the press bulletins, my first thought was that not only my brother and his wife, but also my niece and nephew would soon be able to come and visit us in West Berlin. But when Schabowski, answering a journalist's excited question as to when the new regulations were to come in force, said somewhat hesitantly: "If my information is correct, to the best of my knowledge, immediately," I still could not believe that on the evening of that very day the first East Berliners would come across the border to West Berlin. The GDR Council of Ministers and the Politburo had neither planned for nor prepared for the border to be opened in this fashion. But after these press bulletins, the Berlin Wall had suddenly become superfluous.

This is what many souvenir hunters from East and West Berlin must have said to themselves when, in the third week of November 1989, they began breaking out and putting to one side fragments of the superannuated wall. The section of the wall standing near the Brandenburg Gate was a particular favorite, as is documented by the following photographs. By the time a crossing point was opened there, one short month later on December 22, to the applause of tens of thousands of Berliners, the wall in that area was already as "holey as a Swiss cheese."

The border between the two Germanies and the Berlin Wall lost all meaning in a short time, even before the politicians in the two Germanies had completed their preparations for reunification. On June 26, 1990, the last defense minister of the German Democratic Republic, Rainer Eppelmann, ordered a stop to all border controls. In September 1990, two weeks before German reunification, the GDR border troops were dissolved and the remnants incorporated in the FRG Bundeswehr (army). The official razing of the Berlin Wall in Bernauer Straße had already begun in the summer of 1990.

East and West Berliners gather at the wall at the Brandenburg Gate after the opening of the border in the night of November 9-10, 1989. Un-armed GDR border troops are standing on top of the wall . The banner reads: "If the wall stays, the people go, if the wall falls, she is bankrupt, yes, it is truly hard for our poor GDR" – 11th November 1989.

Together, East and West Berliners celebrate the opening of a new temporary pedestrian crossing at the Brandenburg Gate –
22nd December 1989.

Opening of the border crossing at the Brandenburg Gate. Front row 2nd from right: FRG foreign minister Hans-Dietrich Genscher, FRG minister Rudolf Seiters, the President of the Berlin legislature Juergen Wohlrabe, second row from the 4th right, the FDP leader Otto Count Lambsdorff, the chairman of the CDU fraction in the legislature, Eberhard Diepgen, FRG minister Dorothee Wilms, Mayor Walter Momper and FRG Chancellor Helmut Kohl – 22nd December 1989.

*The provisional border crossing for pedestrians at the Branden-
burg Gate – 12th January 1990.*

"Wall pecker" talking with border soldiers of the National Peoples Army on Ebertstraße – 12th January 1990.

The Archives of the Land of Berlin

The Archives of the Land of Berlin assists citizens in answering the most varied historical, legal, scientific and genealogical questions. As the central state archive of the Land of Berlin, it is responsible for conserving, processing and making available the historically important documents produced by the authorities of the Land of Berlin. These documents include the dossiers, official documents, maps, blueprints, and computer data that are produced by the Senate, the city district councils and their subordinate services. In addition, the Archives of the Land of Berlin receives and collects personal collections, panoramas, posters, photographs, theater programs and other documents concerning contemporary history, including sound and video recordings in so far as they are relevant to the history of Berlin. The Archives of the Land of Berlin promote understanding of the history of the city through publications, exhibitions and conferences.

The Publications of the Archives of the Land of Berlin

Twenty-fifth Anniversary Jubilee Volume: Berlin in Geschichte und Gegenwart. 25. Jahrbuch des Landesarchivs Berlin 2006, edited by Uwe Schaper, Berlin 2006.

ISBN 978-3-7861-2537-2
25,- Euro

Includes:
– Eckart Bergmann: Das Concert-Haus in Berlin, Leipziger Straße 48.
– Nic Leonhardt: Im Bann der „Bühnengefahren". Preußische Theaterverordnungen zwischen Prävention und Subversion.
– Annette Thomas: Rudolf Mosse. Ein Medienzar im Kaiserreich und sein gesellschaftliches Umfeld.

– Volker Viergutz: Der Hahn-Jügens-Block am Alexanderplatz. Zur Planungs- und Baugeschichte des Geländes vor dem Georgenkirchplatz.
– Bernhard Sauer: „Goebbels Rabauken". Zur Geschichte der SA in Berlin-Brandenburg.
– Helga Staudenraus: Adolf Blumberg (1876-1941). Das Ende eines jüdischen Lebens in Berlin. Aufzeichnungen des Journalisten und Publizisten Gerd Tolzien.
– Kerstin Bötticher: Die Verwaltung der Kriegssachschäden in der Reichshauptstadt Berlin 1943-1945.
– Dietrich Steinbeck: „Nennen Sie mich getrost einen ollen Striese". Zum 100. Geburtstag des Theatermenschen Boleslaw Barlog.
– Werner Breunig: Matthias Koeppels Bilderzyklus „Abschied der Moderne. Who's afraid of the Brandenburg Gate?"
– Werner Breunig: Berlin-Chronik 2005.
– Sabine Preuß: Das Theaterjahr 2005. Premieren der Berliner Bühnen.
– Volker Viergutz: Jahresberichte 2004/2005 des Landesarchivs Berlin.
– Inhaltsübersicht und Register der Jahrbücher 1982-2006.

The annals of the Archives of the Land of Berlin for the years 1995 and after can still be obtained in the bookshops. The complete table of contents and index for the annals

1982-2006 can be consulted on the website of the Archives of the Land of Berlin. Serial publications of the Archives of the Land of Berlin, edited by Jürgen Wetzel, continued by Klaus Dettmer and Uwe Schaper:

Bd. 1

Teil I-IV, Das Landesarchiv Berlin und seine Bestände, bearb. von Heike Schroll und Regina Rousavy, Berlin 2003-2006.

Bd. 2

T. I und II, Die Sitzungsprotokolle des Magistrats der Stadt Berlin 1945/46, bearb. und eingel. von Dieter Hanauske, Berlin 1995 und 1999.

Bd. 3

Günther Schulz: Stadtpläne von Berlin 1652 bis 1920, Berlin 1998.

Bd. 4

Günther Schulz und Andreas Matschenz: Stadtpläne von Berlin 1652 bis 1920. Tafelband, Berlin 2002.

Bd. 5

Heike Schroll: Spurensicherung. Die Bestände des Stadtarchivs Berlin und ihr Schicksal durch den Zweiten Weltkrieg, Berlin 2000.

Bd. 6

Benedikt Goebel: Der Umbau Alt-Berlins zum modernen Stadtzentrum. Planungs-, Bau- und Besitzgeschichte des historischen Berliner Stadtkerns im 19. und 20. Jahrhundert, Berlin 2003.

Die Vier Mächte in Berlin

Beiträge zur Politik der Alliierten in der besetzten Stadt

Herausgegeben von
Michael Bienert · Uwe Schaper · Andrea Theissen

ISBN 978-3-9803303-1-2

19,90,- Euro

Bd. 7

„Es wächst zusammen, was zusammen gehört". Beiträge zum wissenschaftlichen Kolloquium zu Ehren von Jürgen Wetzel am 25. November 2003 im Landesarchiv Berlin, Berlin 2004.

Bd. 8

„Die gemeingefährlichen Bestrebungen der Sozialdemokratie", T. I: Die Berichte der Regierungspräsidenten über die sozialde-mokratische Bewegung in den Regierungsbezirken Frankfurt/Oder und Potsdam während des Sozialistengesetzes 1878–1890, bearb. und eingel. von Beatrice Falk und Ingo Materna, Berlin 2005.

Bd. 9

Die Vier Mächte in Berlin. Beiträge zur Politik der Alliierten in der besetzten Stadt, Berlin 2007.

Bd. 10

Stadtpläne von Berlin. Geschichte vermessen, bearb. von Andreas Matschenz, Berlin 2006.

Bd. 11

Polizeipräsidium Berlin. Politische Angelegenheiten 1809–1945. Sachthematisches Inventar, bearb. von Rudolf Knaack und Rita Stümper, Berlin 2007.

Landesarchiv Berlin
Eichborndamm 115-121
13403 Berlin-Reinickendorf

Telefon: (0 30) 9 02 64-0
Fax: (0 30) 9 02 64-201
Internet: www.landesarchiv-berlin.de
E-Mail: info@landesarchiv-berlin.de

Wieland Giebel (Ed.)

BERLIN – DAMALS UND HEUTE
(Berlin – then and now)

96 pages, 11 inches by 9.4 inches, hardback
19,80 Euros
ISBN 13: 978-3-929829-48-8

The metamorphosis of a city:
Old Berlin was almost entirely destroyed by the Second World War. This large-format book of photographs of "Berlin, then and now" invites you to go on a voyage in time of a particular sort: Dive into the historic, pre-war city – and surface in the new Berlin!

Over 40 significant spots in Berlin and their history come alive -- photographed from practically the same standpoint. These fascinating and in part practically unknown photographs show the face of the old and the new metropolis. There is an explanation in four languages (German, English, Spanish and Italian) of each photograph.

WWW.BERLINSTORY.DE

Peter Frischmuth

BERLIN KREUZBERG SO36

96 pages, 8.3 x 8.3 inches, Color- and b/w-photographies, hardback
19,80 Euro
ISBN 13: 978-3-929829-68-6

A world-wide success story: Peter Frischmuths impressive work – a side-by-side comparison of Kreuzberg SO36 Berlin with pictures from 1982-2006 – has recently been on a world tour. The exhibiton has been displayed throughout Germany, in 10 American states and is on its way through Russia, China and Ecuador.

The success is easy to explain: Frischmuths photos take the observer back to the time of the wall and back again with two contrasting pictures: the wound is healed, the wall has gone! A moving portrait of the western front line, which has since become the heart of the city.

WWW.BERLINSTORY.DE

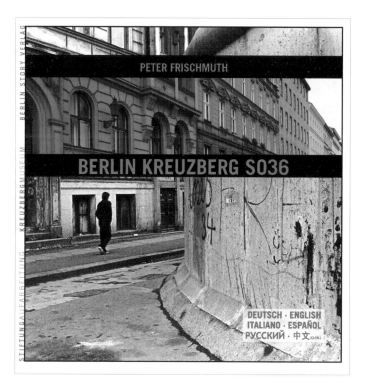

Photo credits

The Archives of the Land of Berlin:
pp. 12 re, 40 re, 41, 76, 110 re; **Wolfgang Albrecht** pp. 55, 74, 119, back cover; **H. Bier** pp. 60, 91, 108; **Dieter Breitenborn** pp. 34, 98, 100; **Ludwig Ehlers** pp. 9, 52, 62, 83, 89 left, pp. 94, 120; **Max Jacoby** p. 54 right; **Edmund Kasperski** pp. 77, 103, 121-123; **H. Knöpel** p. 82; **Peter Kühnappel** p. 12 left, p. 80 left; **U. Kubisch** p. 102 left; **D. Lohse** pp. 50, 72; **Ingeborg Lommatzsch** pp. 115, 116; **Helga Mellmann** p. 44; **B. Röhl** p. 69; **Bert Sass** p. 14 right, pp. 20, 58, 66, 70, 90, 105, 106 left, p. 110 left; **Barbara Schneider** p. 113; **Günter Schneider** pp. 63, 75; **Karl-Heinz Schubert** pp. 22, 37, 51, 53, 54 left, p. 80 right, pp. 84, 85, 92, 99, 102 right, p. 106 right, p. 112; **Gert Schütz** pp. 14, 15, 40 left, pp. 59, 93, 97; **Hans Seiler** pp. 23, 46, 73; **Horst Siegmann** pp. 13, 18, 19, 21, 25-29, 31-33, 35, 38, 39, 47, 61, 67, 68, 87, 88, 107, 111, 117; **Johann Willa** pp. 43, 45, 89 right, pp. 95, 101, 109.